CLASSIC Disney Songs

ISBN 978-1-4950-6903-1

Walt Disney Music Company
Wonderland Music Company, Inc.

DISTRIBUTED BY

HAL•LEONARD®
CORPORATION

7777 W. BLUEMOUND RD. P.O. BOX 13819 MILWAUKEE, WI 53213

The following songs are the property of:

Bourne Co.
Music Publishers
5 West 37th Street
New York, NY 10018

BABY MINE
GIVE A LITTLE WHISTLE
HEIGH-HO
HI-DIDDLE-DEE-DEE (AN ACTOR'S LIFE FOR ME)
I'M WISHING
I'VE GOT NO STRINGS
SOME DAY MY PRINCE WILL COME
WHEN YOU WISH UPON A STAR
WHISTLE WHILE YOU WORK
WHO'S AFRAID OF THE BIG BAD WOLF?

Visit Hal Leonard Online at
www.halleonard.com

BIBBIDI-BOBBIDI-BOO
(The Magic Song)
from Walt Disney's CINDERELLA

Words by JERRY LIVINGSTON
Music by MACK DAVID
and AL HOFFMAN

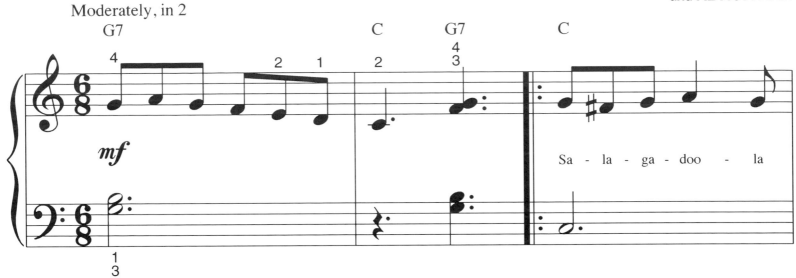

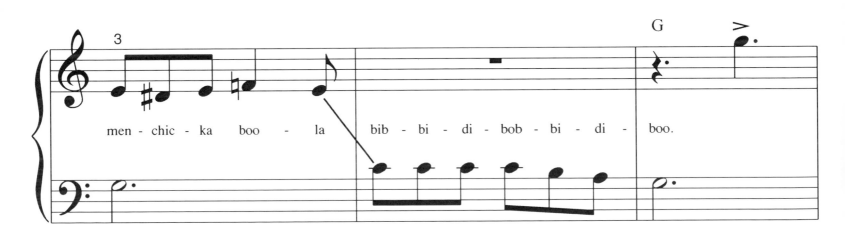

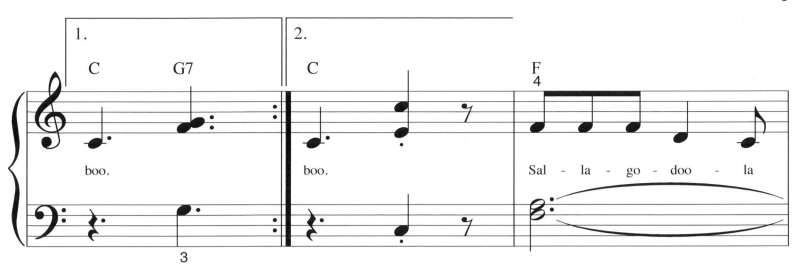

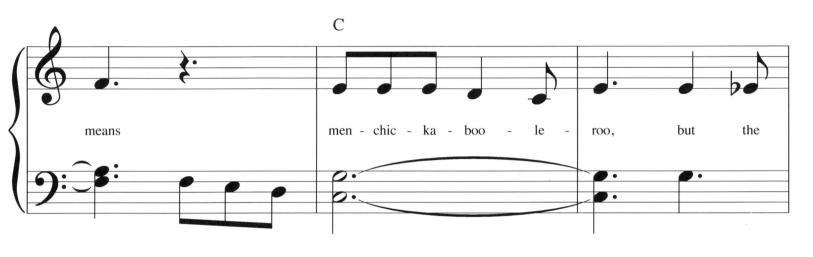

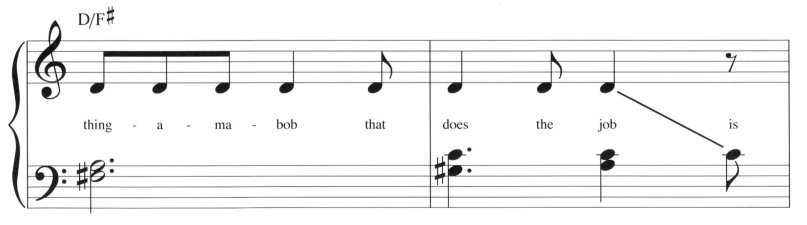

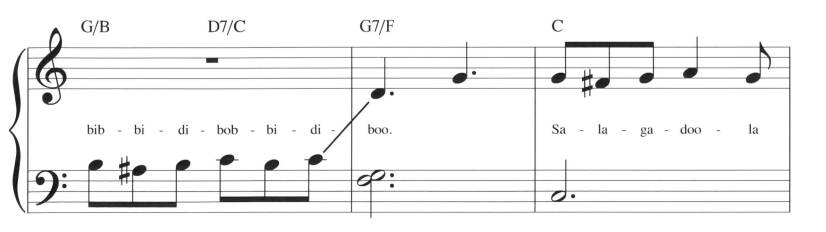

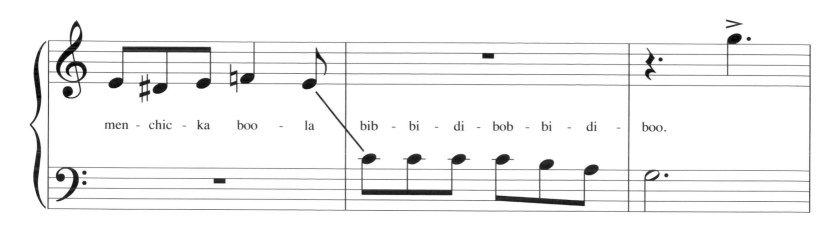

men - chic - ka boo - la bib - bi - di - bob - bi - di - boo.

G7

Put 'em to - geth - er and what have you got?

4

Bib - bi - di - bob - bi - di, bib - bi - di - bob - bi - di,

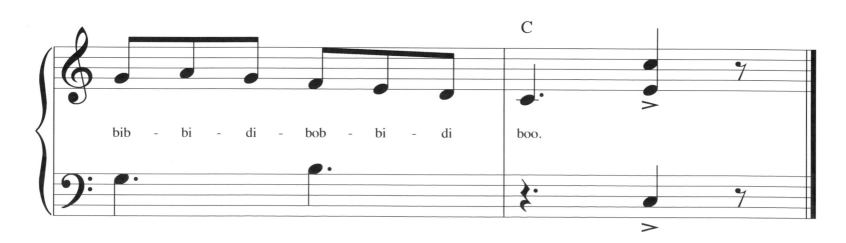

C

bib - bi - di - bob - bi - di boo.

BABY MINE
from Walt Disney's DUMBO

Words by NED WASHINGTON
Music by FRANK CHURCHILL

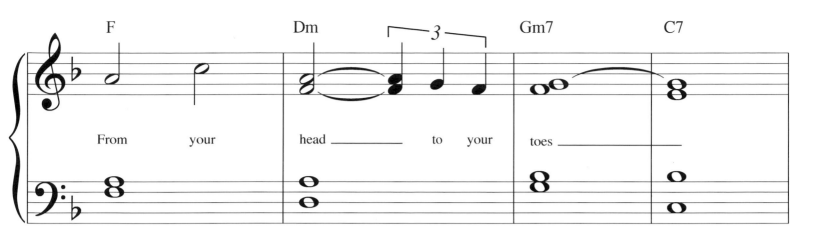

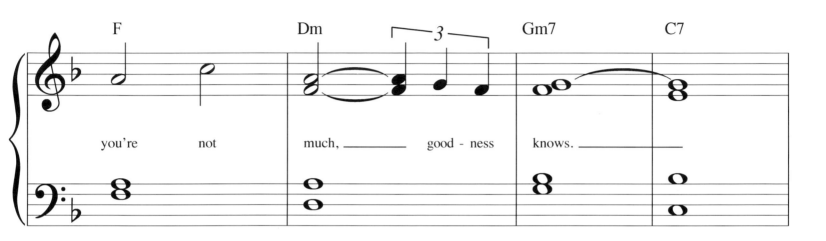

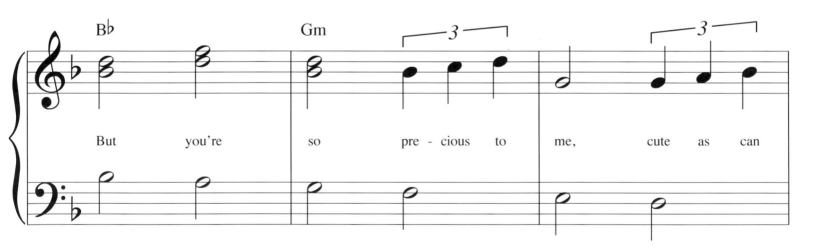

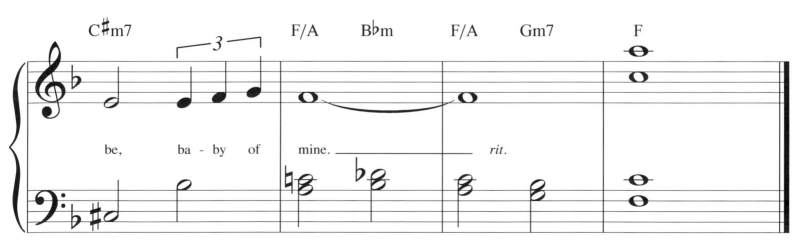

GIVE A LITTLE WHISTLE

from Walt Disney's PINOCCHIO

Words by NED WASHINGTON
Music by LEIGH HARLINE

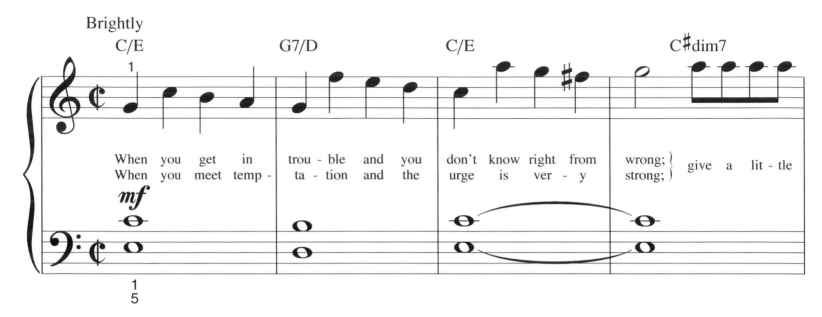

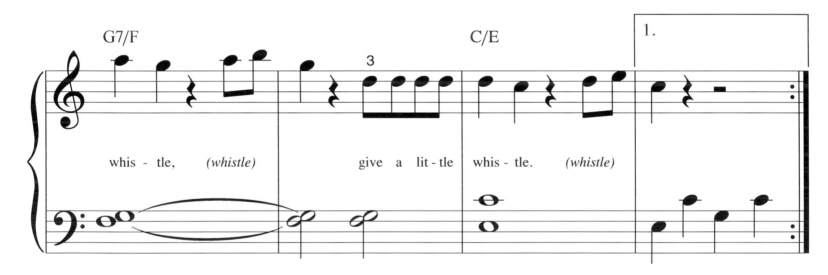

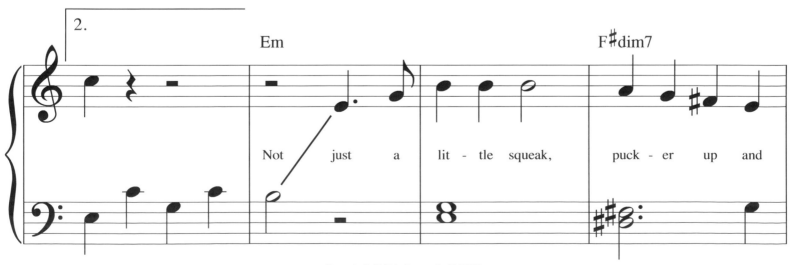

I'M WISHING
from Walt Disney's SNOW WHITE AND THE SEVEN DWARFS

Words by LARRY MOREY
Music by FRANK CHURCHILL

HEIGH-HO
The Dwarfs' Marching Song
from Walt Disney's SNOW WHITE AND THE SEVEN DWARFS

Words by LARRY MOREY
Music by FRANK CHURCHILL

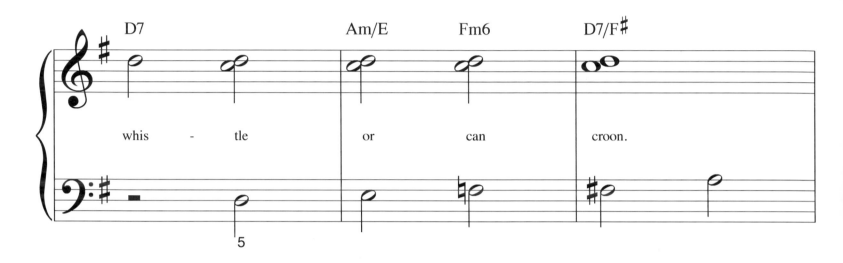

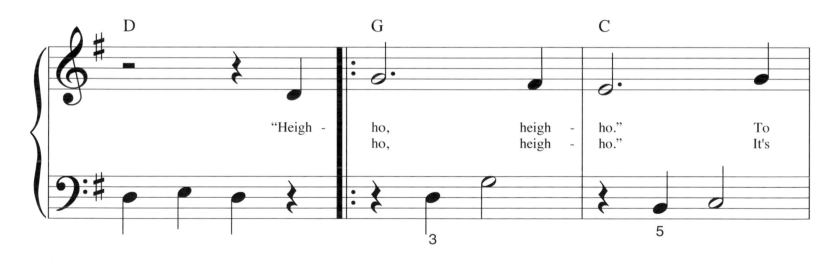

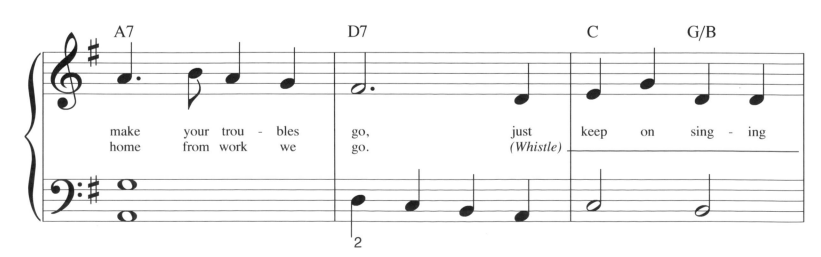

HI-DIDDLE-DEE-DEE
(An Actor's Life For Me)
from Walt Disney's PINOCCHIO

Words by NED WASHINGTON
Music by LEIGH HARLINE

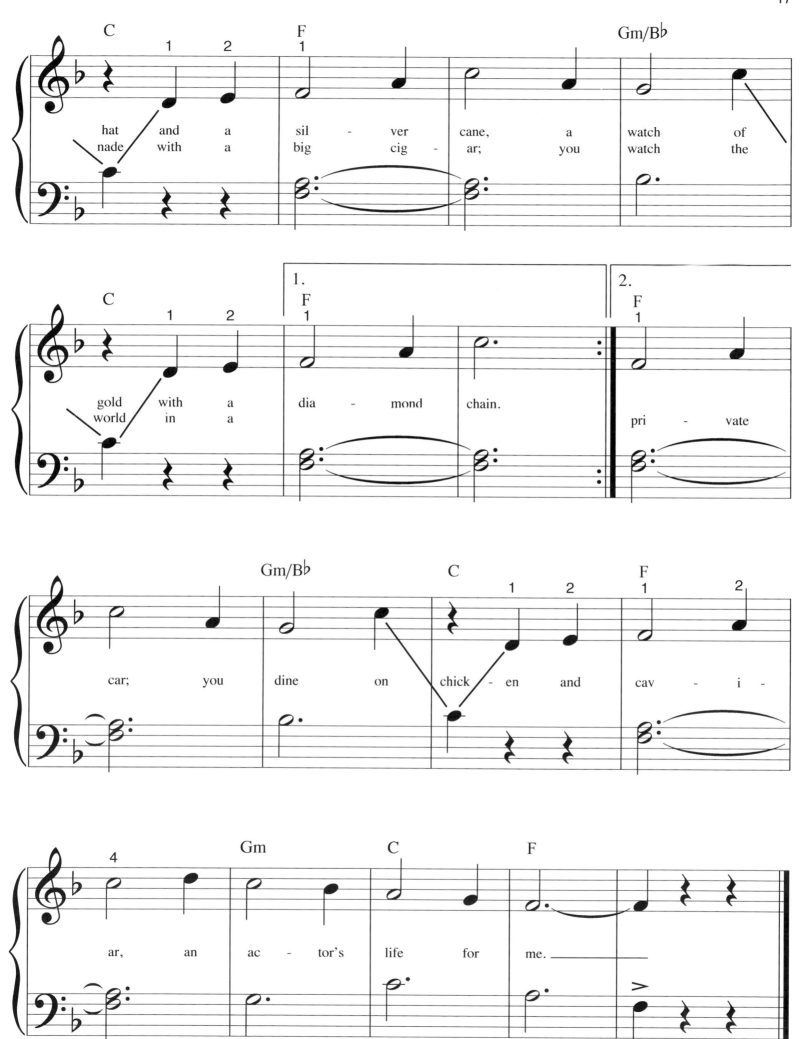

I'VE GOT NO STRINGS
from Walt Disney's PINOCCHIO

Words by NED WASHINGTON
Music by LEIGH HARLINE

19

LAVENDER BLUE
(Dilly Dilly)
from Walt Disney's SO DEAR TO MY HEART

Words by LARRY MOREY
Music by ELIOT DANIEL

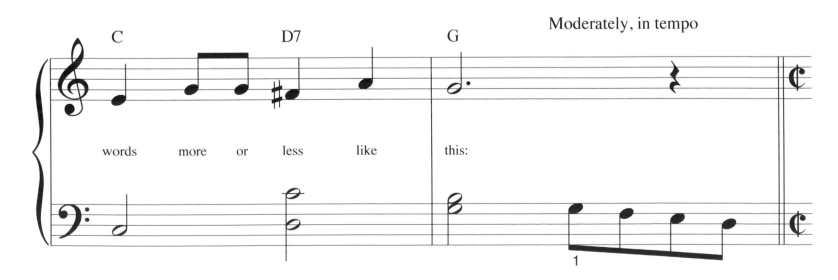

WHEN YOU WISH UPON A STAR
from Walt Disney's PINOCCHIO

Words by NED WASHINGTON
Music by LEIGH HARLINE

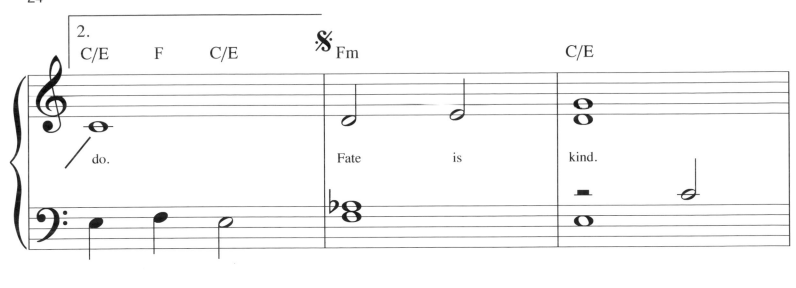

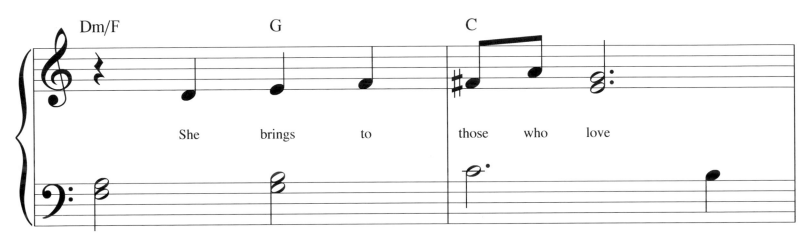

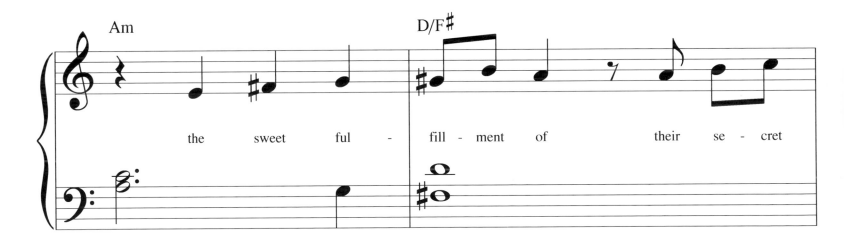

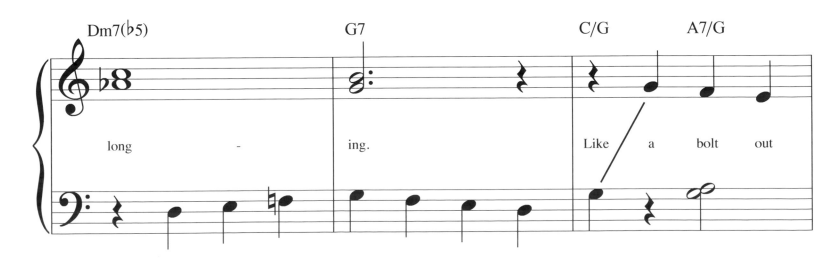

SOME DAY MY PRINCE WILL COME

from Walt Disney's SNOW WHITE AND THE SEVEN DWARFS

Words by LARRY MOREY
Music by FRANK CHURCHILL

WHISTLE WHILE YOU WORK

from Walt Disney's SNOW WHITE AND THE SEVEN DWARFS

Words by LARRY MOREY
Music by FRANK CHURCHILL

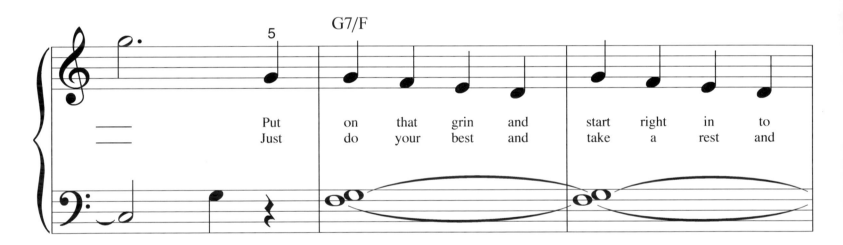

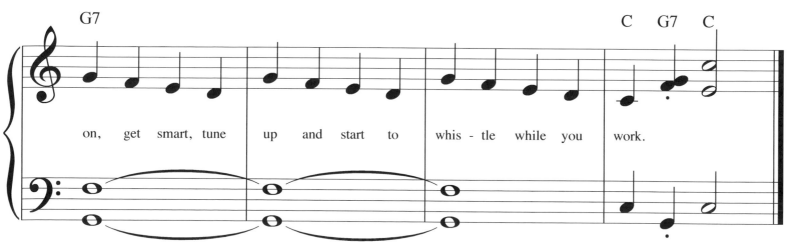

WHO'S AFRAID OF THE BIG BAD WOLF?

from Walt Disney's THREE LITTLE PIGS

Words and Music by FRANK CHURCHILL
Additional Lyric by ANN RONELL

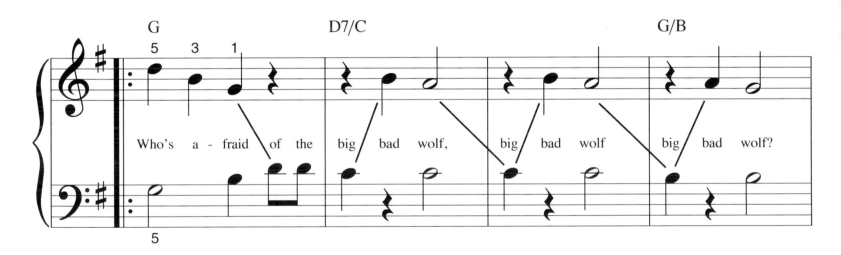

Who's a-fraid of the big bad wolf, big bad wolf big bad wolf?

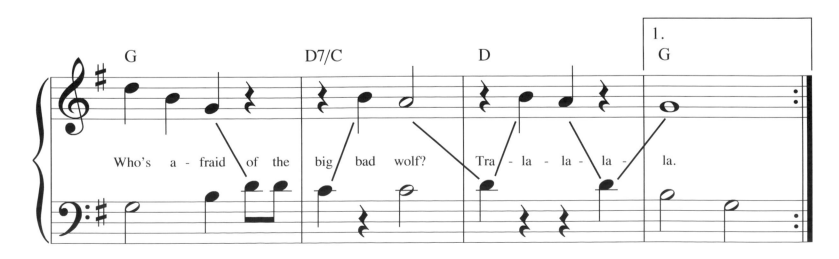

Who's a-fraid of the big bad wolf? Tra - la - la - la - la.

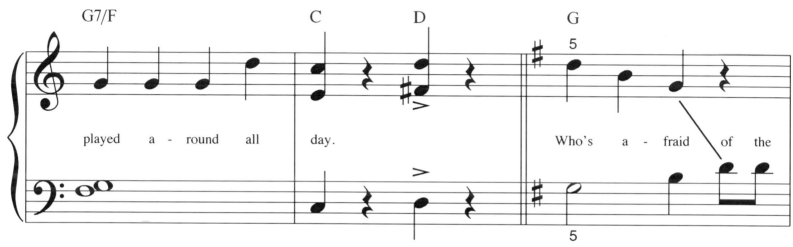

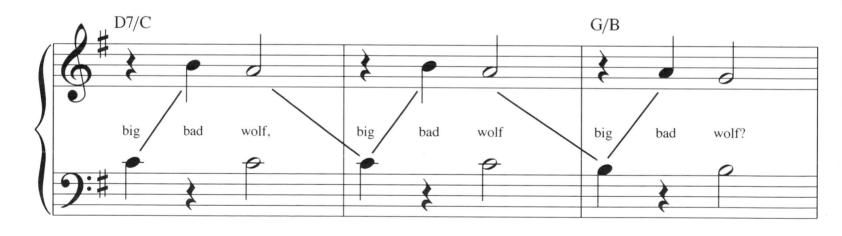

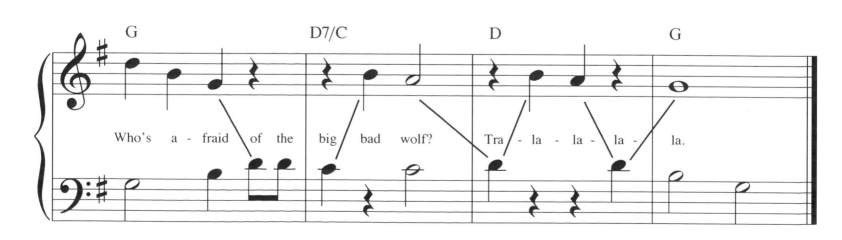